UNREQUITED

One night in April

TONYA WHITTLE

Copyright © 2025 by Tonya Whittle
Cover Image: Debbie Hudson
Cover Design: The Print Shop, Mount Pearl, NL
Publishing Support: Mark Leslie Lefebvre, Stark Publishing

All rights reserved. No part of this publication may be reproduced, distributed, or transmitted in any form or by any means, without prior written permission.

Unrequited – One night in April / Tonya Whittle
Jan 2025

Paperback ISBN: 978-1-7388051-2-9
eBook ISBN: 978-1-7388051-3-6

Dedicated

To G
For that one night in the Bahamas
April 27, 2024
That changed my life
I long for what might have been if I hadn't been scared
And yet I am grateful for the locks that fell off my heart
Because of it
I will love you forever
Platonically
Divinely
Intimately
For eternity
Whether I see you again or I don't
I will hold you in my heart
And find you in the stars

Holding Back

"I want to stop holding myself back" I whispered to my Friend.
"I don't know why I have all these rules of engagement" I added.
How long?
How much?
Who?
Where?
What?
When?
"So jump in" she yelled back.

Walls

I'm not good at this.
These walls are high. Impenetrable.
I don't know how to let people in.
I want to. And I don't at the same time.
I want to know love.
Deeply.
As deep as I feel it inside of me.
And yet I don't know how to open up.
I'm safe here.
Behind these walls.
Uncaring.

Collision

Somehow, that morning,
I collided with you.
I decided I was ready.
There you were. Inviting me.
As you said "come enjoy the show then come with me"
Confidently.
Not an order as much as a statement.
A fact.
It wasn't an ask. It wasn't audacious.
Just knowing. And stating.
Me brave or naive or both.
I had never done this.
Not the one night stand.
Not with someone in another country,
Or someone famous.
It was like a dream.
Shrouded in a veil.
"What is happening" I yelled.

Windy

The wind whispered all night.
As it blew through my hair while I danced.
I said yes.
I'd meet you.
But I wasn't sure I would.
I was numb.
Not because of this.
But because of everything.
I didn't know how to feel anymore.
Maybe I was searching for more.
Life. Passion. Something.
To make me feel alive again.
I'm just some girl from the East Coast,
I told you.
You're someone who knows the
People I stream.

Unworthy

Why would you choose me? I asked.
"Damn you're gorgeous" you said.
As I filed it away.
Not believing it.
I spent the last twenty years begging to be enough.
And here you were making me feel more than enough.
Tread carefully, I reminded myself.
As I downed another drink.

All In

You talked so flippantly about me visiting you.
Going on tour with you.
I nodded. Not saying yes or no.
Changing the subject.
Acting aloof.
Because I didn't really believe you.
My past is filled with men who say what they think I want to hear.
Plus,
People wanting something from me, scares me.
Even you.
Especially you.

Intensity

But it was building.
There was more.
Vulnerability.
Instantly.
Shared snippets of life.
Grief.
Love.
Joy.
Passion.
Comparing tattoos.
Laughing intently.
It was as if the room fell away.
The sounds of the casino drowned out.
The crowd around us somehow quieter.
And all I could hear was you.
The intensity was building.
Of desire.
Of everything.
Conversation.
Vulnerability.
I felt seen.
And that scared me.
As we closed the bar down.

Just One Night

Walking away
You took my hand.
People stood aside.
Staring as we walked by.
All I could think was I had to ask
To have my hand held, before
As he walked in front of me and I struggled to keep up.
While you stayed with me, ensuring all
Who walked by knew I was with you.
I wasn't sure what to make of this.
I felt safe.
And I never feel safe.
Like a wild animal backed into a corner most of the time.
Feeling safe scared me more than feeling frightened ever did.
This was just one night, I reminded myself
This was nothing.
I was just another girl in a long line of girls.
Have fun and let it go.
Don't read into this
You're not mine, I told myself.

Deep

"You wouldn't know what to do if a man treated you right,
Would you?" you asked.
Looking in my eyes
I felt it in my soul.
As the elevator doors closed behind us.

Intense

15 floors.
I wasn't sure we would make it.
Clothed.
Hands everywhere.
In your hair.
Lips on my neck.
Glass reflecting it all.

Catching My Breath

I can't breathe
As we back into the room
Your hands on my lower back
Me biting your lower lip
Sucking in your bottom lip
The air left my lungs
And I couldn't get it back
I struggled to catch my breath
As you backed me in
Is this really happening, I wondered.

You Vs Me

I felt the stark transition
From my own life
To this life
You had just performed for thousands
Have performed for tens of thousands
Maybe hundreds of thousands
And I did things
But mostly I walked my dogs
In the woods
And wrote books
How am I here
In this place
With you
How do you not compare me?
When all I do is compare me.

Comparison

Sitting on the bed
You pulled me in between your legs
Asked what I was thinking
I asked you
"Why me?"
"Don't you have a million groupies?"
"That gets old" you said
"I'm looking for something real"
 "I don't even have work done
And you're around all these ... not me"
I blurted out
Why am I like this, I thought...
Arguing for my own rejection.

Surrendering

As you slid your hands up my sides
Exposing my black lace underwear
Standing up
Eyes locked
As you peeled my dress off
"Damn you are finnnnneeee"
As his voice rung out in my head
"You let yourself go"
As you pushed me back against the bed
"Can we turn the lights off" I asked
"No I want to see you and you to see me"
As you trailed down my stomach
Lower
And I gave in
No holding back
Succumbing to the emotion
Letting myself be good enough
Even if for just this moment

Worshipped

It's unnerving to meet a man who wants
A woman to be more
Where I can be smart
And sexy
Not either or
Most see women as a body only
Ignoring all other parts
And those who pay attention to the
Other parts
Miss the body
A woman wants to be whole
Met in her power
Respected for her mind
And worshipped for her body
It's a fine line
So few know how to walk
Asking a woman to be her whole self

Ravished

Because I want a man
I can show up in lingerie
And be treated like a bombshell
Not a bimbo
I don't want to pack up
Who I am
Over and over
I want to show up in boots
Lift me on the counter
While I wrap my legs around you
Ravished.
Then read a book,
Have a real conversation
About stuff that matters
Is that too much to ask?
For it all?

Weaponized

Women are not only whores or virgins.
Though we're written that way.
Life is too short for bad sex and
Shitty relationships.
Where we're weaponized.
Demonized.
Where men see us as one or the other
One to play with
The other to marry
Not knowing that
We're all those things.
We all want meaning.
And depth and passion and purpose.
And we want to be all of that.
Because we are all of that
When we're allowed to be.
Not many men can awaken a woman
And love her wholly.
As she is.
Without asking her to be half of who she is.
To be wanted
One needing just the body
Another needing just the mind
When we want all of it.
Never satisfied.

Whole

You could be him.
That I long for.
Or you could represent him.
Showing me it's out there.
Available.
Possible.
Some men can handle whole women.

Green Flags

All green flags.
Before during and after.
As we lay exhausted, hours later.
You fell asleep, quickly.
I stared at the ceiling.
I didn't ask if I should stay or go.
I didn't know if I should wake you.
Or not.
I crept to the patio.
And watched the lights glistening on the bay.
How am I here?
With him.
I wondered.

Conflict

I crawled back in next to you.
Creeping my hands along the tattoos on your chest and arms.
Intertwining my hands.
Letting my guard down for a moment.
It was safe.
You were asleep.
I did the girl check "I'm leaving soon" I said.
"Just let me know if you decide to stay so I know" my Friend said.
So flippantly, as if sleeping over was a thing.

More Walls

I don't sleep over.
I reminded myself.
And yet I wasn't in a rush to go.
Absorbing I guess.
The entire thing.
Who he was.
Where I was.
Another country.
All of it.

Guard Down

I woke up hours later.
You were still sleeping.
But you had moved.
And somewhere in the rising dawn,
Panic rose.
Something took over.
As I scrambled out of bed.
Finding my clothes.
Then my bag.
And before I knew it,
Running.
From the room.
Through the hotel.
Across the casino.
Clearly misshapen.
An epic walk of shame,
To onlookers.
But something more to me,
I cannot explain.
Terror.
As I crawled into my own hotel bed.

Regret

Regret consumed me.
I ran.
Like I always run.
Mostly figuratively.
This time literally.
No goodbye.
No wake up.
Nothing.
Just vanished.

Why?

"Why would you do that?"
"Imagine if it was done to you?" My friend asked.
"I don't know how to stay", I replied.
It wasn't a conscious choice.
I just reacted.
Staying over is...
I'm afraid I'll be unwanted in the morning.

Protecting Me

And I shrunk even more
I wasn't trying to hurt you.
I was trying to not hurt me.
I didn't think you'd care.
That I would do you a favor.
I'd be gone.
Save you the trouble.
I wasn't thinking,
It wasn't conscious.
It was action,
Triggered by fear.
Of rejection.
Humiliation.
I was told repeatedly I wasn't enough.
How was I supposed to believe that I was enough for…
Someone like you?

Self-Sabotage

I had an opportunity.
For the very thing I dreamed about.
But never admitted to anyone.
I didn't believe I deserved it.
Or I would get hurt.
So I left first.
Too afraid to believe.
Too afraid to want.
Too afraid to see myself
As he had clearly seen me.
Too afraid to see my own worth.

Wanting More

The realization dawned on me.
"I wanted more" you texted.
Breakfast. A walk. Get to know you more.
Messages flashed across my screen.
Rapid fire.
Why can't I just admit what I want, too?
Why this cool facade of not caring?
Why all this self-protection?
I know why.
Where it comes from.
But will it ever end?
What if I just said what I wanted to say?
What if I just admitted I have feelings?
That I'm human.
That I want things I'm afraid I can't have.
I try not to want them,
So I don't long for them.
Reject them before they reject me.

Home

I want to be the one you come home to.
Not necessarily you.
Maybe you.
You're a representation, I've realized, of what I want
That I deny myself.
But someone.
Who wants to come home to me.
And I want to come home to them.
Safe from the world.
Not a war together.
But an oasis from the wars out there.
A safe place to land.

Love

I want deep love.
But everyone says it's too soon.
They don't know all that I ever had was surface.
And I've always longed for something deep.
Why so many rules for the heart?
Why let the head rule in matters it doesn't understand?
Is it too soon when you meet someone who can take you where you've always known you were meant to be?

Stay

Why am I so afraid to express my feelings?
When it was so easy for you?
I just shut them off as if it wasn't real.
Why is it so hard to say…?
I want this.
I want you.
I want to stay.
I want to try.
Even if it fails.
To run to something that lights me up?
Instead of running away.

Unrequited

Why do we say Taylor Swift or Post Malone,
Or every song ever written is poetic,
Of unrequited love.
Of professing our feelings to each other.
But in real life we hold back.
Or if we do,
We fear we're labelled.
Crazy.
Too much.
Too soon.
Too fast.
So we bite our tongue.
Hiding love.
And creating masterpieces of tortured hearts,
That cry out, for each other.
Afraid to show up in life.
And only show up in writing or
Music or art
Where it's…
Palatable instead of arrestable.

At first sight

Is love at first sight real?
Is it possible to be so deeply moved and changed by a
Fleeting meeting?
Can 7 hours do that much to someone?
I worry I'm crazy.
But I worry more I'll never get a second chance.

Soul Love

Love at first.
Or soul at first witnessing?
Maybe it doesn't matter.
Something shattered in me.
And I know that no matter what,
I was meant to meet you.
It's not about you.
It's about you showing me
The cage in which I insist
On living.

Power

The point of this is power.
Take my power back.
A woman cannot be in her authentic power,
With a weak man.
Who likes her powerless.

You

I will never listen to drums again,
Without a catch in my heart.
A moment of regret.
And sadness mixed with love.
A sad and happy smile,
At the same time.
For you gave me something back that someone else,
Took away.

Need No One

We're taught not to need anyone.
To reclaim ourselves alone.
And that can be powerful.
But what if we've got it wrong?
That we need someone else to give back what was taken?
If we didn't throw it away,
How is it ours to find?
Maybe we need someone to show us,
We can trust, we can love, and we can feel,
Again…
Maybe it's ok to need someone.

Finding God

Through you I met God.
And through God I met myself.
Finally, ready to drop a mask.
A story.
Of a girl who doesn't care.
But cares deeply.
In a world that loves surface.
I learned to stuff my depth away.
And apologize for my feelings.
And suppress my desires.
But through you and the pain of longing I feel,
I have finally realized and learned a harsh lesson.
In masks and pretending,
Instead of being and asking,
I stand now,
Before God,
Before you
Begging
For forgiveness,
For all that I've harmed,
Mostly myself.
In the belief that I should be other than who I am.
Being deep, in a surface world, hurts.
But darkness and pain are my superpowers.
For there I must find my own light.

Unlocked

I have been sick since you told me,
You wanted more.
But I thought you didn't.
And I left.
In the middle of the night, no goodbye.
Not what I wanted but,
Too afraid to stay.
To be rejected.
Through you I found my depth again.
My words again.
Unlocked.
Like you were the key,
To the places I've hidden me.

Dreaming

Hopelessness embedded me.
It was my security blanket.
Afraid to want.
Scared to dream.
Who I was, lost.
Numbness was my favorite partner.
My big dreams, shuttered.
A cage wrapped around my grieving heart.
But you unlocked me.
Through pain. And regret.
The great awakener of souls.
You brought me back to desire.
To want.
To chase.
To long.
To need.
To dream.

Ache

My heart aches for something I've never had.
That I didn't know was possible.
Or even real.
A fairytale?
But was so close.

I want to know you

I want to know everything about you.
But I gave up that right.
When I snuck out of your room,
In the middle of the night.
Making you think I didn't care.
But I care.
Too much.
I want to know you.
All of you.
My heart …
Hurts.

Losing Love

How can I so deeply ache for someone I only spent a
Few hours with?
I hurt.
Physically.
Is this love.
Or risk of losing love?
Or of unrequited love?

Free Fall

What I want to tell you is how scared I am to love.
How scared I am to believe in someone better.
In someone wanting more,
With me.
How scared I am to trust.
How scared I am to let go.
How scared I am to love.
How scared I am to free fall.
And how scared I am not to …
Because what is life without that kind of love?

Why did I run?

Why did I run away? You asked…
"Because this is all new to me" I said…
But that was a lie.
I ran because I was scared.
Because I felt this fire and it scared me.
I wanted to throw myself into you.
And it terrified me.
I wanted to get lost in you.
And I was terrified I'd lose me.
Now I know I would find me there.

Craving

When your heart and soul know.
Why would you want anyone else to ever touch you?
When my heart aches for one person.
And my body craves just one touch.
One nights feel meaningless.
And yet they're why we're here.

Shrinking

I have been shrinking
Into myself
Into nonexistence
Into not belonging
When I do belong
With him
With them
Wherever I am.
I started to disappear.
To save myself
To be unseen
To shrink
In humiliation
Or fear
Or I don't know.
I don't know why I hold myself back
As if I don't belong
Exactly where I do
Exactly where I am
Why do I shrink to be unseen?
Invisible.
With you, especially.
Why would I not take the space you offered?
As if I were imposing in some way.
As if I didn't have a right to exist.
When all you wanted was my existence.
And I didn't know how,
To take up space.

Precious

Love is too precious to be ignored.
Don't run from it
Run to it
With everything you have
The thing I've been most terrified of
Is the thing that I need the most.
To stop playing demure
To be the Queen I am
To the King I desire

Negotiating

If you don't feel the same
I get it.
It's a lot.
Too much.
I remind myself, constantly, still shrinking.
But for the first time in my life.
I'm more of scared of not reaching for it
Losing it, for sure
I am tired of being scared
Of love
Of commitment.
Exhausted from aloof.
I'm tired of negotiating with love as if it's
A bargaining chip.

Fear

I'm more afraid of not having love
Than sharing what I want.
Finally.
The cage doors are open.
The shackles have fallen.
A key, in a random night.
In a random country.
Of all the places we could have been.
Of all the mornings I decided to be ready.
Of all the people we could have chosen instead.

Holding Back

Are we so conditioned now to hold back?
Or is that just me?
So when you asked me to be your girlfriend,
To travel,
Could you have been serious?
When I've only met men who want to Fuck me…
Or own me…
Who want too much of me…
Or who don't know what to do with me
Who play with me.
Ghost me,
Put me on read.
And for me to accept it,
To play the game.
To not be clear, act like I don't want it
Not be confident about what I want,
Or who I want,
Or how I want it,
For fear of being too much, too aggressive,
Coming on too strong.
You came on strong.
But I thought it was an act,
Because all those before you,
Were.

The Ocean

I've never been honest about my depth.
My friends yes
My mentors
And spiritual teachers
Yes
But never the public
And certainly never a man
Arm's length
Act like I don't care
Because that's what they want isn't it?
Or it's what keeps me safe.
But it isn't true?
I want the depth of the ocean,
Nothing less.

Suppression

I've always talked myself out of my feelings.
Good and bad.
Suppression.
And now what if I don't talk myself out of it.
What if I stop talking and start feeling.
What if it's not attachment theory?
And unhealthy.
What if it's love, actually?
What if we really do just know?
And then all of our stuff gets in the way.
And we run from what we need to run to?

Time

I wanted more time.
That's the thing about running.
It's hard to run back.

Speak Up

What if I tell you?
And you're too angry?
Too jaded?
Don't want it or me?
What then?
It will still be worth it.
Because if there's anything worth risking.
It's for love.
And if not love, self-expression at the very least.
I risked my life and my heart for safety.
Why not for the possibility of love?

Silent

I haven't really told anyone.
Truthfully,
I don't want to tell anyone.
Because I don't want it to be about who you are.
I don't want this to be reduced to a hot night in.
It was.
Don't get me wrong.
But it was so much more.
I don't want it to be about that,
Only about what I learned.

Elevate

I found God at the deepest level
I understood I am God too
And all my gifts are God given
And I am entitled to greatness
That greatness lives within me
That all this time I was aiming way too low
I know God brought us together
For a reason
To elevate my heart
And my words
To open me to love
And to big dreams
Knowing it's possible
And I belong here
I deserve more
Then I've ever settled for

Alignment

Everything was in alignment
For more.
To show us
What's available.
The stars aligned everywhere.
In Toronto.
Meeting Steve and Wil
And had an incredible night.
Men who showed us what it is to be witnessed, seen,
Valued and respected.
Treated well.
Maybe our norm wasn't so normal,
After all.
Maybe it was our trauma that made it so.
But maybe there are great men out there, too.

Wake Up Call

I lost so much confidence and power.
Maybe it's grief.
Or Divorce
Humiliation.
I stopped taking up space somewhere along the way.
You were a glass of water.
Thrown in my face.
That asked me to grab me,
And scream life back into me.
To dare to shine,
Instead of shrink.

Taking Up Space

I've been too scared to take up space
To own the space in which I'm in
To have a say in the space I'm in
Because I didn't have it
I couldn't, even when I fought for it
So I stopped fighting for it
Shrunk
Knocked off my axis
Gave my power to someone who didn't deserve it
I hate that he still had that power
When I ran from you

Taking a leap

Taking the leap to tell you
Is choosing to live in my authenticity
Instead of my attachment
It's releasing fear and opening to power
To cross the barrier
To transcend space
To say this is me

Waiting

I have hung back
Waiting
To be given permission
But
It's only me that can give me permission
I know that now
It's me that has to stay
But I don't know how

Risk

I realize now
I have to say it all
To stop suppressing
To practice
Without fear
Of the outcome of being told no
Of being rejected
Of letting go of control
It's certainty I've been seeking
Keeping myself safe
Fear of losing everything
Instead of,
Risking everything for something that matters

Nothing to Lose

And so what holds me back?
Still.
Now?
Nothing?
There's nothing left to lose but only something to gain.
Worst case I get my own voice back.
Even if I don't get you.
But it will always be you that triggered me
To take myself…
Back.

Plot Twist

In the plot twist
I needed.
This gave me my power back.
To have realized I dreamed of something powerful.
Might have had it in my hands
And walked away
Hurting you
And me
Regretting not staying
And deciding to redefine myself
Because I never want this to happen again
It's always pain that leads me to power.

Found

That feeling I was searching for
The certainty
The knowing.
The me I used to be. I missed her.
The fighter. The dreamer.
The one who chased her dreams.
It came back.
Through you.
Through this.
You brought me home,
To me.
Brought me back to life.
My soul had been languishing.
Lost.
But now I'm found.

Encounter

How can one encounter
Change your life?
It's like a movie.
Maybe it was the place.
Or the timing.
But it was life changing.
And I won't pretend it wasn't.
I won't cast it off, aloof.
As just another notch on a bedpost.
But this time a deep notch in my heart.
One I will let change me.
Because I need it to.
The only way to have my deepest dreams is to be my whole self.
That means I must stop pretending
Not to care.

Instant

Can love be instant?
Do our souls recognize each other?
And we know?
But our conditioning, reactions, fear and trauma,
Prevent us,
From reaching to each other?
Do we let life get in the way instead of letting love in?

Me

You taught me to reach for me
I touched greatness
And while I might have fucked it all up
It showed me that I do belong there
In all the places I want to be
And that my dreams have always been way too small
What comes from this now
Is that I have the key
To my own greatness
My own success
To dream

Unravelling

You pulled a string
Unravelling me
From the masks I wore
To pretend
To play a role
And unraveled the deepest parts of my soul.
Exposed me
Brought me home
To who I am
What I want
A remembering
A becoming
An unbecoming of sorts
That showed me the cost of hiding myself
Of not being myself
Not being me
Not asking for what I want
And in an instant
Divine intervention
To bring me home to me
And I hope one day to you

Dare

It's that daring
To believe
To dream
To feel
To love
Against all conditioning
And odds
And yet know it's time
To risk it all

Role Play

You play a role, you said
I understand that
I played one for you
I thought you wanted
But you didn't
And I lost
The game of roulette
That we play with love

Sadness

I felt you
So sad
A depth of sadness that felt bottomless
Perhaps lost, too
That I recognized in myself
A safety
A yearning
A longing
That made me lean closer

Protecting Me

I wasn't trying to hurt you
When I ran
I was trying not to hurt me
I saw something
Felt something
And it scared me
I couldn't give myself to another man
Who wouldn't care

Trigger

I thought you wouldn't care
The never-ending story
The stimulus
The trigger
The reaction.
And finally,
A response, too late.

Rewriting It

Maybe it's all moot
Maybe I was right
Maybe it was intuition
Saving myself from pain.
I want to rewrite it again.
Like I always do.
To something more palatable.
But what's the point?
I had that for twenty years
And got destroyed anyway
For nothing
So if not for the chance at love
What else would we risk it all for?

That woman

It's that cycle of conditioning,
All that fear of being too much,
Too soon,
Demanding,
A nag,
That woman,
Don't be "her",
But you're damned if you do and
Damned if you don't.
When you lean in, they lean out.
When you lean out, they lean in.
Everyone loses.
Always.

Pay Back

The bad ones ruin you for the good ones.
The good ones pay for the mistakes of the bad ones.
And you pay for all of it.
Always in some limbo…
Getting it wrong.

Trauma

Trauma
Seems like such a wrong word
But my therapist said
"Don't downplay it"
And I realize that's all I ever do
Downplay it
Me
My trauma
My desires
My needs
My wants
My truth
My power
Because I've believed it, and me, are all too much
And the cause of all of my problems

Ruining Things

When you said you knew what you were to me
I knew
I hurt you
And it didn't feel good
You weren't only that to me
I thought I was only that to you
Why we do over complicate
And ruin everything good?

Stay Small

I let him take 20 years that I can't get back
I can't let anyone else have more of me that I can't get back
I can't let him have anymore
He didn't want all of me
He wanted just the shell of me
Robotic
Sit
Stay
Shut up
Be smaller
No, smaller still
You're nothing
No one
And there was you
Wanting all of me
But all I could hear was him.

Second Chances

I'm not saying I deserve a second chance.
But I want one.

The juxtaposition

It feels like I was slapped in the face.
I gave a million chances to the wrong people.
And even the right ones,
Who make mistakes.
I forgave, easily.
But I was never given the same opportunities
To be forgiven
Or fought for
Just doors slammed in my face.
Anytime I didn't get it perfect,
The first time.

Shattered

And I finally stopped running, for a moment
When I realized it was just me I was running from
Because I had listened to
The signs. Your words
Dared to believe
A man like you, would want a woman like me
Two different worlds
But the same heart
It all sounded too good to be true
And instead of reaching for it
I let it slide between my fingers
Shattering at my feet
If I break it first
It can't break me

Don't Want More

Don't want more than I have, I thought
One night is enough.
But then my heart joined the glass on the floor.
Shattered.
The cost too high.
For the safety of fear.

It's me, I'm the problem

It's not physical
It's my soul
Whether I ever see you again or I don't
You unlocked a door inside me
A cage door opened
A wall fell
The ice melted
As I saw myself
On my knees
Facing myself
That it is me
Holding me back
Safely choosing the wrong men
Fearfully rejecting the right ones
Conflict
Between head and heart
No matter what
You led me back

Solving a Mystery

It has to be bigger than me.
Something.
Because I wouldn't have faced this
Stayed pretending
I wouldn't have given myself grace
If I had not been broken open
To solve a mystery I had been chasing
Like a dog with its tail
Around in circles
'til I was dizzy.

Soulmate

A soul mate comes to bring you home to the highest
Version of yourself
It's not always romantic.
In fact it's often destructive.
I was playing so small
Pretending
Playing a role
Wearing a mask of not caring
Not letting myself care
But you brought me
To a place nothing else could
And for that I'm grateful.

Before We Met

I have had this dream
My entire life
A place I lived inside of myself
Where I hid from the world
A self-protection
Where I believed
Dreamed
Deeply of a man
Who wasn't like the others I met before
A man who desired me
Cared about how I felt
Who held my hand
Opened to me
Fought for me
To open me
To trust him
And I did
And I realized when I hurt you
That it was you
Him from my dream
A representation of him
I dreamed of you long before I met you
But I shut the door behind me
Sneaking out
The difference is
You didn't come for me
You let me go
And I knew
It was never your role
His role
Anyone's role
To save me
From myself

The Taylor Version

We write love stories? Rom coms and serendipity and
One Night in Paris and songs about unconditional love…
Love at first sight
People and experiences that change us
Forever
And not really believe in them
Regaled them to fantasy, fairytale
But we grew up on them
Hoped for them
It's why Taylor and Travis are such a hit
It's not just pop culture
It's not fandom
It's a living fairy tale
When a guy pursued her
Put himself out there
Really really out there
She saw him
And the end
Love
We're promised it
But were so god damn afraid of it
We want the Taylor version
But we settle for the "realistic" version
The one the world told us is safer
To get our head and hearts out of the clouds
So we do
But then we miss
The shot we didn't take
We long for the stars
But settle for the earth
Too afraid to fly

The Prince

Is it crazy?
Or is it just me?
Is everyone else honest about what they want up front?
Or are we all just playing roles?
Pining for something we were raised on then told it
Doesn't exist.
Are we still hoping the prince will reach the turret window?
And save us from ourselves?

Reaching Out

What do I have to lose?
If I reach across time and space?
To you?
And what will it cost me if I don't?
Because even if you say no,
Am I not, bravely, finally, saying yes to me?
Regardless of you.
You were never the point.
Only the catalyst.
For me to see that I am the one,
Who needs to say what I want,
Instead of shrinking from it.

Being Brave

Isn't it brave?
With no certainty.
But to express myself
To open the door
Even if you close it.
To have been brave enough
To stop suppressing myself
To tell you how I feel
And let you decide,
How you feel.
Knowing this isn't about you anyway
But giving myself the right to exist
And what I want to exist.
To ask for what I want
To desire something and be brave enough to risk
Everything for it
Knowing I'll be ok
Even if you don't choose me.
Because what is mine also wants me.

Broken Pieces

I felt brave,
Once,
Not broken.
But I was shattered into a million pieces.
But somehow this pulled all my
Broken pieces,
From the floor.
I discovered my heart was beating still.
This stuffed it back inside of me.
And I am reminded that really,
I have more to lose if I don't go for it.

Outcome

The outcome is less important,
Than the courage to try.

Divine

Somehow this is spiritual.
All this pain.
Led by God.
Because nothing else opened me to love this way.
Not just external love.
Not romantic love.
But internal love.
Eternal Love.
Divine love.

Writing My Way

My writing protects me from my feelings.
Makes me look braver than I am.
Cloaks me in fearlessness,
To say,
What I cannot express.
But I've never shared my deepest words
Because they go against the persona I've created.
You can't pretend not to care,
If your writing is always in the deep end.

Yours

You wished me luck with finding someone better
Than you.
Why would I even look?
My soul knows what it wants.
Why would I let anyone else touch what's yours?

Gilded Cages

I've wanted out of this cage forever.
To stop pretending.
You freed me in seven hours
When someone else imprisoned me for twenty years and
Made it look like freedom.
A gilded cage is still a cage.

Change

I don't want to keep making the same mistakes.
Over and over again.
The only way out
Is through.
To avoid repeating
I have to do something different
And express myself.

Expansion

I shrunk
Instead of expanding.
If I expand
And I'm too much
It's not the right space.
When I want to shrink to fit
I must remember to expand
And outgrow.

Romance

Why do we see the notebook as so romantic?
But in real life messaging someone for a year makes you
A stalker?
She didn't know he was,
She wanted him too,
That's the difference, I guess.
But why is my limit two messages,
And then disappear forever?
Terrified of being labelled as "one of those" women.

Sidelines

I take myself out of the game before you can reject me
I reject myself
I reject you
To protect me
I don't get involved
And instead sit on the sidelines
Wishing I was playing.

Hunger

We ignite our hunger
On romance novels
Then feed ourselves
On empty connections
Wondering why we never
Feel full

What Must Die

You killed the part of me that needed to be killed.
Something that needed to die within me.
And I am grateful for that.
But I wish it hadn't killed,
Our connection in the process.

Softness

There were moments
I recall
A tenderness
A general interest
In the pain of each other
As you looked at my tattoo of Lexie
And wanted to know about her
You didn't shame me for my grief of her
As you shared your loss
And your regrets about it
As we momentarily moved between tragedies and
Traumas in the most fleeting moments
Captured by the soul of us
Connecting
To be replaced
In the early morning
Light
With
Fear

Tolerating

Before this
I didn't know how to ask
That I could ask
That I should ask
I could express myself
Say anything
Other than vanish into myself
I tolerated from men the lowest
Asked for nothing
Gave the highest
And I assumed you were the same
Maybe you are
I'll never know

Hypnosis

There was something hypnotic in that night
In the feeling
I find myself wondering if it was real
But I know it was
I felt it
More than physical
In a place no one had ever been before

Like The Rest

I showed you things
That night
Earlier
Softer
That I never showed anyone else
I felt safe enough to fall asleep
I had never done that
But then
When I woke up
You, away from me
Instead of wrapped around me
I froze
Like the rest
Years of begging for love
I ran

Writing another Story

I thought I was another
Notch
My heart disconnected
From what I knew
The sadness I felt from you
And I thought I was just one of many
A line long
I like to write my walls back in place
So I never know what's truth
And what's story

Sadness

I'm deeply and incredibly sad
I want to reach across the ethers for you
But I'm scared
I wish I never knew you wanted more that day
This is exactly what I was trying avoid

Dulled Down

Is love something we should settle for?
Dulled down?
Shrinking?
Should we settle for what's safe?
Or should we chase blindly into the abyss?
Is it better to live without it?
With a half love
We aren't afraid of?

Locked Doors

What you saw
Was someone who rejected you.
But what you didn't see,
Was that I was stopping me from being rejected.
Underneath it all
The pain
The layers
The fear
There is an ocean of love
That I cannot open the door to.

Honesty

And yet,
As scared as I am to open the door.
I must.
I'll never again live without being honest.
About my feelings.
About who I am.
And what I feel.
Or what I want.
It's not worth the price.
You open your heart.
And the truth comes out.
It cost me too much closing.
And I'm not willing to risk that again

Recovery

I ran
Not to hurt you
But to not hurt me
And in the end
I hurt me and you
For I know
Why you would say no
I would do the same
But aren't we just human beings?
Trying?
To recover from all the stuff we didn't ask for?

The Stimulus

Victor Frankle says
There is a space between the trigger and the stimulus
Where our power to respond lives
The key is to find that space
However minuscule
And expand it
That's where our power is
But I didn't find it until it was too late
My reaction to the stimulus
I couldn't see
Triggered me running
I've been running a lifetime
And it wasn't until it was too late
I was in the elevator
The casino
The cab
My hotel
Before I questioned what I had done
If I made the right choice
Knowing I had not

Belonging

I left because I didn't know how to stay
To feel wanted
To belong there
To take up space

The Letter

You might not want to hear from me but for the first time
In my life I have to be brave enough to say what I
Feel and stop pretending I don't care when I care
Deeply all the time.
I didn't meant to hurt you. I was trying not to hurt myself.
I don't sleep around. You were my first date in twenty years.
I've been single since my divorce last year. By choice.
I Never met anyone I wanted… until you.
I felt something for you … in the bar … I felt it when you said
you play a role for people… and when you reached
Across to touch my tattoo of Lexie and when you told me
about your dad. I felt a softness between us…
But when I woke up I felt if you wanted me there you would
have curled into me. That I would have woken up
Tangled in you.
And I reacted. I was out the door before I knew what I was
doing. But what I really wanted was for the entire thing to
slow down, to crawl in next to you and wake up next to you.
I left, not because I didn't want to stay but because I
Told myself it was stupid to feel something for a guy I
Couldn't have.
Finding out you didn't want me to go still hurts… I've never
been treated right by a man. Not my ex. Nor
The men before him.
I'm sorry that I reacted the way I did. It wasn't you. It was all
me but not why you think. I was scared. I'll always
Regret leaving the way I did but not our night together.
I really did have a great night, until I ruined it.
I wish you nothing but massive success and the deepest
Love that exists

The Reply

Babe,
You are amazing. Our night was incredible.
I've thought of it often.
I get it.
I do.
And why can't you have me?
We're just flights apart.

Free

I told you,
Brave in love for the first time, ever.
And it really didn't matter you replied.
I felt free.
Something inside of me let go.
I knew I would always speak up from now on.
No longer voiceless or suppressed.

Cavalier

We pretend not to care
To save face
Cavalier
Instead of laying ourselves bare.

Unbroken

Here I am - open
Not broken
Not where you found me
But where you left me
Without your knowing
Wide open
And open isn't as scary as I thought
In fact, it's the opposite
Without walls
Without the lies
Fear or conditioning
I am free
I can see
The truth
And feel the space
And here I am safe
Because it's me I needed
And you unlocked the cage
Showed me what I could have
Even if it's not with you
Our souls will be forever entwined
In some ether
In a time and place
That God aligned
To get me unbroken

Self-Rejection

It's not protecting ourselves
From love
That hurts us
But protecting ourselves
From ourselves that hurts
More than anything
When we realize we have
Rejected ourselves.

Glimmers

And if there is even the
Slightest chance at having even
a glimmer of it all
Isn't it worth it?
To chase it unabashedly.
To not half live in mediocrity
But to embrace life,
And squeeze every drop.
Chase every glimmer,
Unapologetically.

Not Easy

I'll never be the easy choice.
I'll never be the one that makes it all easy and simple.
But I'll always be the one who is worth it.

Is Love Lost?

Is love lost?
In a surface world have we lost the plot on love?
Billions on love
Romance
Dating
Matching
Playing the game
Leaning in and holding on
Romeo and Juliet
Star crossed lovers
We once pined for
Lonestar's "Amazed" replaced with "WAP"
As we throw love around.
Ashamed to be soft.
More gangster than girl.
Walking through hell made us hellfire
And damnation
Tired of being Queens to men
Who are not Kings.
I wonder if it's like Jesus
We pray to him for him
But if he came now
He would be medicated and institutionalized.
As we sit in pews
Praying for him to save us
Is love the same?
Those who seek it?
Are also too afraid of it.
So we chase it in the most unloving ways.

Suppressed

I couldn't be myself with him
So I don't know how to be myself anymore
When you wanted me
I didn't know how to give you, me
So I gave you what I thought you wanted
Which is what he wanted
And I hate that he did that to me
That he took my past
And my present, too
That I think all men want
The version of me he did
…
Suppressed

Even Walls Fall

Finally
My walls
Are falling
And
I want to keep them down

Self-Rejection

It's not about you
But what you represent
Who you were for me
A sledge hammer
A cold glass of water in my face
To realize that I don't choose me
Before anyone else can not choose me
Self-rejection as self-protection

Wrong Spaces

Maybe it's never been about anything other than that.
For me to stop suppressing me.
To stop swallowing down all of who I could be
To be invisible
To be unseen
As if I don't deserve to take up space in someone's life
As if being unassuming
Leaving
Not demanding or asking for what I want
Will be more pleasing
To those who are wrong for me anyway

Unlearning

Unlearning
The way I have lived
To find the trigger before it destroys me
To awaken to the depth that's available for me
Because why wouldn't someone choose me?
If I chose to love myself I could see
How much I bring to the table
And I deserve just as much in return
No more one sided
You showed me just how much I'm worth
My insecurities
Bred, and fed, by weak men

Running To

I have to learn to stay.
Let them reject me if they will.
But never to reject myself again.
Instead I want to stop holding myself back.
I want to run blindly into what I want.
Knowing that what I want can only find me that way.

Purpose

Maybe some relationships are just what they are.
A lifetime in seven hours.
It's not about us.
But what we represent in the snap shot of time we had.
More depth than I had in twenty years.
My softness for you only grows.
My gratitude is massive.
For my soul came back to my body that night.
I remembered and reclaimed me.
I'll always see us fondly,
Even my mistakes,
I see through a lens of forgiveness.
I love you.
In all lifetimes.
I will love you forever
Platonically
Divinely
Intimately
For eternity
Whether I see you again or I don't
I will hold you in my heart
And find you in the stars
Because you gave me something
Someone once stole from me.
You looked at me like I was worthy.
When others made me feel worthless.
And I'll always be grateful for you,
For that.

Fortune Favors the Bold

Rejection wasn't what happened
Made up in my head
Worse case scenarios
That's the thing about vulnerability
And fear
And needing certainty
Above all
But fortune favors the bold,
After all.

Risk & Reward

Sometimes the scariest thing
Is opening
At all.
Sometimes when you're willing to fall
You're caught before you do.
The biggest thing to fear
Is fear itself.

Possibility

"Hey babe…
Did you know…?
We're in London on the same day?"

What's the chances?

Also by Tonya Whittle

Unchained: A Journey To The Soul From Head To Heart

Unchained is a soul-awakening account of life after childhood trauma, of one woman choosing to let go of who she thought she was so she could become who she was meant to be.

Tonya Whittle's story reflects what happens to so many women when they pretend trauma didn't happen: who they become, what they do, and how they create a vision of themselves for protection. But what happens when the life someone is running from collides with the life they've created? *Unchained* shares Tonya's own journey through the collapse of a life falsely created, exposing her wounds and forcing the truth. Tonya encourages other women to take off their own masks, face their truths, and do the inner work necessary to live life fully, ultimately leading to healing and rebuilding.

Unchained takes women on a journey to the soul, from head to heart, from fear to faith, from girls gone wild to wild soul women. For anyone who feels disconnected from life, who is just getting by, simply existing, Tonya reaches out to encourage them to let go of the things that have happened to them and thrive despite those traumas. In the face of #metoo and #timesup, her story serves as an instruction manual for how ancient wisdom, and the process of facing the past, lead to an amazing future—no matter what happened.

Also by Tonya Whittle

Relentless: Life with Labs
Life Lessons From Woman's Best Friends
An Unforgettable Love Story

This is a remarkable story of a life well lived because of dogs. Join Tonya as she shares the lessons she learned from raising and adventuring with her two chocolate labradors, Tetley & Lexie. Unlikely gurus on life, unruly and wild, Tetley & Lexie come to life on the pages as their explorations outside lead to powerful lessons in how to live life well.

During their countless adventures, mishaps abound, they bring us to laughter and tears with their antics and larger-than-life personalities. Blended together with stories from everyday life, Life With Labs explores how dogs teach us to be better people.

Wild, heartwarming and insightful, Life with Labs is a modern love story explored through the unbreakable bond between a woman and her dogs as they embrace an unconventional life.

> *"It's like the Thelma & Louise of dogs but stops just before you go over the cliff, letting you write your own ending. I loved every moment of this book."*
> —Nancy Burton

www.ingramcontent.com/pod-product-compliance
Lightning Source LLC
LaVergne TN
LVHW041255080426
835510LV00009B/749